Stepping Through History

MONEY

PEGGY BURNS

Wayland

Stepping Through History

Money
The News
The Post
Shops and Markets
Travel
Writing

Series editor: Vanessa Cummins
Book editors: Marcella Forster and Vanessa Cummins
Series designer: John Christopher

© Copyright 1994 Wayland (Publishers) Limited

First published in 1994 by Wayland (Publishers) Limited
61 Western Road, Hove, East Sussex BN3 1JD, England.

British Library Cataloguing in Publication Data
Burns, Peggy
Money. – (Stepping through History Series)
I. Title II. Series
332.409

ISBN 0-7502-1135-0

Picture Acknowledgements
The Publishers would like to thank the following for allowing their pictures to be used in this book: The Bank of England 19 (above); Bridgeman 9; British Museum 11, 13 (above), 22 (below); Camera Press cover (top), contents, 13 (below), 16, 18 (below); Chapel Studios 24, 25, 28; Coutts Bank 20; Mary Evans 22 (above), 27; Eye Ubiquitous cover (left), 17 (bottom), 18 (above); Robert Harding 10 (below); Michael Holford 10 (above); Image Select title, 24; Impact (McCaig) 15 (above); Peter Newark 6 (below); Photri 12 (inset), 17 (inset), 25 (below), 26 (above), 28 (above);Royal Mint 14; Ronald Sheridan 6 (above), 8, 12 (below), 27 (inset); Skjold cover (main picture); Survival International (Englebert) 7; Wayland Picture Library cover (right), 4 (below); Werner Forman Archive 23; Zefa 26 (below), 29.

Typeset by Strong Silent Type
Printed and bound in Italy by G. Canale & C.S.p.A., Turin

CONTENTS

WHAT IS MONEY?

Everyday we use money to buy food, to travel to work, paying bills, using the phone or going to the cinema. It would be very hard for us to live our lives without money.

So where did money come from, and who invented it? And what, exactly, is money?

Wherever you live, coins are handy for buying the smaller things you need.

We use money to buy everyday things such as fruit and vegetables from a market stall.

In a few remote areas of the world, people do not use money at all. There are no shops so things are exchanged, such as animals or pots, with friends, neighbours and other traders. However this is very rare.

For most people, money is coins or banknotes, or cheques, that are accepted in payment and exchanged for the goods they want. This is known as buying.

Currency from around the world.

Money, whether paper or coins, in itself is not worth very much. It is the things that you can buy with money that make it of value.

There are many different types of money around the world. Most countries have their own type. Each is known as a currency.

LIFE BEFORE MONEY

What do you think life would be like without money? Like most other things, money wasn't always around. It had to be invented.

Flint arrow heads like this one were popular as items to barter with.

Thousands of years ago trading was only done by exchanging goods. You would offer your spare produce such as vegetables or cloth to somebody who had cooking pots to spare. If you were lucky they would need your produce and give you some of their pots in return. Exchanging goods in this way is known as bartering.

Bartering has been with us for a very long time – it was first recorded in ancient Egypt 4,500 years ago. People began to make sure they had something to spare to barter for the things they needed; they grew extra grain or vegetables, or wove extra cloth.

Native Americans exchanging furs with the early European traders probably for metal tools.

These men from the Yanomamo tribe in modern Brazil are discussing what to barter.

In Britain around 3500 BC, flint was used for barter. The flint was valuable because it was made into axes, weapons, and simple farm tools. Small, rough pieces of flint were used and exchanged for animal skins, pottery and food.

However, there was a problem with bartering. For instance, if you wanted to exchange grain for wine but the wine-trader did not need your extra grain, you could not barter with him directly. You would have to find a second trader, who needed some grain, barter with him for some goods the wine-trader did want, and then exchange them for the wine.

This was very complicated and made bartering awkward, because first of all you had to agree how much each object was worth.

Ancient Egyptians took care of the herds of cattle that represented their wealth.

As time went on some objects became more popular than others in the bartering system. People liked to have lots of cows or grain to make sure they wouldn't go hungry.

Cattle became symbols of wealth and instead of saying 'How much does it cost?' you might have asked, 'How many cows is it worth?' A family was thought to be rich if it had large flocks of sheep and herds of cattle or goats. The animals became an early form of money.

EARLY TRADE AND THE FIRST MONEY

An ancient Egyptian trading vessel.

As far back as 2000 BC people of different countries were travelling hundreds of kilometres to trade with each other. They set up what were known as 'trade routes' – well-known routes from country to country. They crossed deserts, mountains and seas carrying goods made in their own countries to exchange for foreign goods.

Camels being used to carry goods across the desert in the nineteenth century.

Traders from Crete and Greece carried olive oil, pottery and metalwork, and exchanged them in Egypt for beautiful alabaster vases and other Egyptian goods.

The Romans took oil, wine and wool from what is now Italy to Africa and the East, and brought back spices from Arabia, gold from West Africa, grain from Egypt and North Africa, and silk from China.

In Britain precious metals were mined and exchanged for luxuries from the rest of Europe. Because barter was such an awkward way to buy and sell, it was seen that something else was needed to trade with. It had to stand for the flint and the goat, something which symbolized the goods being traded.

Money was invented and came into use in many different countries at around the same time, 2000 BC.

Native Americans used lengths of wampum beads sewn together as money.

Fourteenth-century Chinese paper money representing one thousand coins.

Many different things have been used as money since then. At first cowrie shells were used in China, and later in Thailand and India. Large stones were used by the people of Yap, an island in the Pacific Ocean. Paper, which was precious because at that time it was very rare, was first introduced as money in China. In Fiji, whales' teeth were used and Native Americans used wampum beads made from shells.

All these things may seem rather strange to us now but they were familiar and valuable to the people who used them in the past.

CARD MONEY

Money to pay the French soldiers stationed in Canada in 1685 had to be shipped over from France. Shipments were often delayed and money became scarce.

Below: Playing cards were still used in 1791 when money was in short supply.

Above: The back of the playing card was signed by the governor to prove it was money.

The government began to use playing cards, marked with a certain value and signed by the governor, as money. Playing card money was used for more than one hundred years.

HOW COINS WERE FIRST USED

One of the earliest known developments in the invention of coins occurred in Mesopotamia (now known as southern Iraq) around 2000 BC. Pieces of silver, of a measured weight known as a shekel, were used to pay for goods. The weights were not sealed or stamped as coins were.

Above: A gold bar. The stamp guarantees its weight and quality.

Silver is formed in veins that run through the rock. In this form it is known as ore.

The very first coins were produced in Lydia (now known as Turkey) around 600 BC. They were pieces of metal known as electrum – a mixture of gold and silver – roughly stamped with a seal on either side guaranteeing the weight.

Soon the idea spread to Europe and the Greeks began using round silver coins in Athens. At around the same time coins were invented in southern Russia and Italy.

As more metals came into use, and gold and silver were mined from the ground, precious metals became used more and more as money.

An electrum coin from Lydia, stamped on both sides.

Metal could be cast in any shape and coins were not always round as they are today. In Thailand and Nigeria metal rings were used and in China money was made to look like miniature tools or swords. Metal was even cast in the shape of cowrie shells.

By 100 BC Rome had become the greatest trading nation in the world. With the expansion of the Roman Empire many countries were introduced to gold and silver coins for the first time.

This coin was minted in Rome between 134 and 138 and shows Emperor Hadrian.

Gold made very good money for many reasons. To start with, it is beautiful to look at, so everyone wanted it. Gold also doesn't tarnish or go rusty, as some other metals do. It is a soft metal so it can be hammered out and divided into small and useful pieces. Also it is quite rare because it has to be dug from deep mines.

Gold and silver came to be widely used for coins of high value. Copper and bronze, more common metals, were used for 'small change' coins.

After the fall of Rome, around AD 450, Roman coins gradually went out of circulation. By the year 700 the British were making their own coins, but money was used less than it had been. Rich people's wealth was the gold and jewellery they owned rather than money in the form of coins. Ordinary people needed little money as they lived on what they produced for themselves.

Above: The metal from which coins are made is melted in a very hot furnace, at around 1,000 °C.

Since the invention of coin presses in 1660 coins have been made by machines. Metal bars are heated and squeezed by rollers into thin strips, from which blank coins are punched out by machine. The blanks are then fed into a powerful press, which stamps a design on both sides of the coin at once.

Left: A modern coin machine like this one can punch out over 600 coins per minute from metal strips.

GOLD FEVER!

Gold has always fascinated people. In ancient times it was made into fabulous objects of art, including jewellery, statues, goblets and vases. Unlike other metals, such as copper, it never loses its beautiful gleam.

Below: James W. Marshall was the first to discover gold in the Sacremento Valley, California in 1848.

Above: These beautiful statues, which form part of the Grand Palace in Bangkok, are made from real gold.

In 1848 a man called James W. Marshall was building a mill for his boss on the banks of the Sacramento River in California, USA, when his eye caught the sudden glitter of gold in the gravel of the river.

The news spread: 'If you want to get rich, go to California and dig for gold!' By the following year the world was in the grip of gold fever. Thousands made their way to the

Gold prospectors in California in 1848 used long wooden sieves to sift gold deposits from the river sands.

Sacramento Valley with their spades and gold panning equipment. Some came by ship across the Atlantic from Europe. Risking conflict with Native Americans, they crossed the country in creaking covered wagons, hoping to make a fortune in the new goldfields.

In 1851, gold was found in the Australian outback, too, and the same thing happened all over again. People rushed from all over the world to be the first to stake their claims and get rich.

Many did become rich. But many more found nothing at all, and some even starved to death when their money ran out.

As time went on the need to mint coins outstripped the amount of gold being produced in the world. People began to realize that coins were merely symbolic and did not have to be valuable in their own right. As long as everyone accepted the coins in payment for goods there was no need for them to be made out of real gold.

Gold is now considered too precious to be made into money. Most is stored away for safekeeping. Nearly half of all the gold mined in the Western world lies inside Fort Knox – the world famous deposit for gold – in the United States.

Silver is also too precious. 'Silver' coins are now made from an alloy of other metals, and only look like silver. The alloy is a mixture of copper and nickel.

South African gold mines can be more than 3,500 metres deep.

The Fort Knox Gold Depository.
Today gold coins are only minted for special occasions. For instance in Canada a gold coin was minted to celebrate the 1988 Olympics.

BUYING THINGS WITH PAPER

A pocket full of coins can be useful when you are buying small things, such as icecream or a comic book. But if coins were the only kind of money, you would have to hire a delivery truck to carry them all, if you were buying something big such as a house or a car.

A girl pays for goods using paper money.

HYPERINFLATION IN GERMANY

At the end of the First World War, prices in Germany rose so steeply that paper money became almost worthless. By 1923 workers were being paid twice a day, and they had to use laundry baskets or large boxes to carry home their pay. A loaf of bread cost hundreds of marks to buy. During one year, the German mark dropped by one tenth of its original value. The runaway price increases came to be known as hyperinflation.

Hyperinflation led to great hardship for the people of Germany.

The weight of coins and the fear of having them stolen was always a problem. In China paper money was used instead as early as the seventh century. Marco Polo, the Italian trader and explorer, wrote about it in the thirteenth century. Though his writings were published in Europe, it did not catch on. At that time, Europeans could not see how a piece of paper could be used to buy goods.

It was not until the sixteenth century that Europeans discovered paper money for themselves. A merchant would store his money with a

The first paper money in China was used around the year 600.

goldsmith, who would give him a handwritten receipt which promised to pay back the money when it was needed. The merchant could use the receipt to buy goods from another trader, who would then use it to get the money back from the goldsmith.

A seventeenth-century goldsmith.

In the same way a man who wanted to travel from, say, Rome to Paris, could go to a business man in Rome, who had an office in Paris, and give him some money. In exchange he was given a note which promised that when he reached Paris, he would be given money at the Paris office.

It was much easier and safer to carry paper notes than bags or boxes of gold and silver coins. After a while, the pieces of paper issued by the goldsmiths began to be used instead of coins. As long as all the parties trusted each other paper worked as money.

Some goldsmiths started to form organizations called banks which specialized in issuing notes worth a certain amount in gold or silver. The first bank in Europe to print its own paper money was the Swedish Stockholm Bank in 1661. Each note represented a hundred dalers or silver coins.

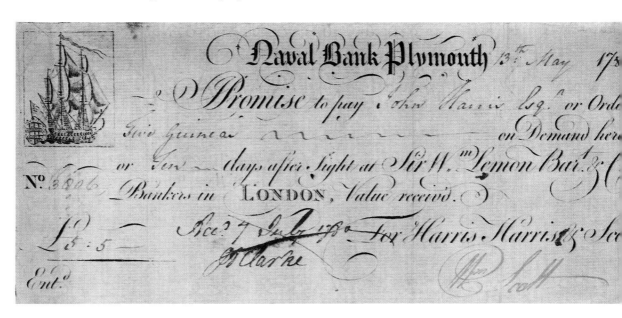

An early example of a banknote produced in Plymouth, England in 1780.

BEAT THE CHEAT

There have always been rogues in the world. Soon after coins were invented, people began trying to find ways to get more money for themselves by cheating. It was not long before they discovered that if they chopped the edges off gold coins they could sell the pieces of gold.

So milling was invented to avoid this. Tiny grooves were cut all around the edges of coins, so that people would know straight away if a coin had been tampered with. Milling is still used today on more valuable coins.

When paper money came into use, greedy people soon began to copy, or forge the notes. An American five-pound banknote issued in 1759

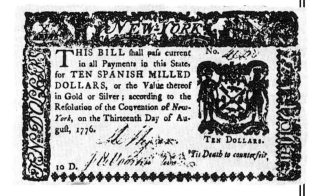

This ten-dollar bill used by European settlers in the USA in 1776 warned 'Tis death to counterfeit.'

warned forgers that they risked the death penalty. In nineteenth-century England you could be hanged if you even owned a forged note.

Forgers are still at work today, and authorities around the world try to keep one step ahead of them.

Milling is still used on coins today to prevent forgery. Milling also helps blind people to identify coins by touch.

This nineteenth-century banknote is a clever forgery.

Banknotes are designed to be as difficult to forge as possible. Ornate lettering, intricate patterns and special inks make it very hard to copy a banknote exactly. Special paper, which often contains coloured fibres, is used. Banknote paper usually has a watermark - a design pressed into the paper itself when it is made. You can see a watermark by holding a banknote up to the light. Metal strips are often inserted into notes for extra security.

Dr Dodd, an eighteenth-century clergyman, was a notorious forger. He was arrested and later executed in Newgate Prison, London.

WAR FORGERIES

Just after the Second World War ended in 1945, villagers living near Lake Traunsee in Austria were delighted to find hundreds of English banknotes floating on the water. They were forgeries. During the war the Nazis had produced 140 million pounds' worth of forged notes. They had intended to flood Britain with them, hoping to make people distrust British money – any note they received might be a copy. Only a small number of notes reached Britain.

THE BEGINNING OF BANKS

Money lenders and goldsmiths soon realized that as people used more and more paper money the gold in their stores never actually moved. It was just the paper promising to issue the gold that changed hands not the actual gold itself. This meant that the goldsmith could lend a little of the gold out and make money by charging the borrower for it. This was the beginning of banking.

The first bank opened in Amsterdam, Holland, in 1609. By the mid-seventeenth century banks had become commonplace in Europe. Banks could also be found in Japan where they were run by feudal clans or temples. Temples issued their own paper money as well as holding religious services.

This temple is in Kyoto, Japan. Japanese temples issued their own paper money.

A bank that had failed, London 1882.

To stop this happening today most governments make laws to control how much money a bank can lend out. In Britain the government set up the first central bank, the Bank of England, in 1694. Banks still fail from time to time, but not as often as they did in the past.

How would you go about saving to buy something expensive, such as a computer or a mountain bike? If you were wise, you would open a bank account and take your money, week by week, to the bank, until you had saved enough to buy what you wanted.

A modern French bank.

Many of the early banks went out of business because they lent out too much gold. When people came to collect their own gold there wasn't enough to go round. This became known as a 'run on the bank' because people would literally run to be the first in the queue to get their gold back. Many people lost their entire life savings.

Today there are banks in every city and town in the world.

A bank keeps your cash safe for you. When you put your money in an account, you are lending it to the bank. The bank pays you a certain amount for lending them your money. This is called interest.

Modern bank interior.

But where do banks get the money from to pay interest? They earn money by borrowing from some people and lending to others, charging interest on the money that they lend out. The person who borrows money, perhaps to buy a house or a car, has to pay back more than he or she has borrowed.

The interest that banks take from people who borrow from them is more than the amount they give to those who lend them money. That is one way banks earn money.

So you can safely put your savings away in your bank account and know that some day you will get your money back – with interest.

PLASTIC MONEY

Most of us are familiar with the idea of credit cards. The first credit cards were issued in the USA in the 1920s by large oil companies and hotel chains to help people pay for their goods and services.

After the Second World War, plastics were developed and used to make all kinds of household goods. Plastic money, too, was invented. Credit cards such as Access, Barclay-card, American Express and many others, are now widely used instead of 'real' money. People who have credit cards can use them to pay bills and buy goods all over the world.

ATMs give out money night and day.

International credit cards.

The cards can also be used in automatic teller machines – ATMs. Card owners are given a PIN (personal identification number) by the bank, which they tap into a keyboard on the machine. The machine won't work without this special number. These computerized machines can be used to get cash from a bank account, or find out how much money is in the account. Most banks now have ATMs.

MONEY AROUND THE WORLD

Most countries today have their own money, or currency. The coins and banknotes all look different and most of them have different names. Occasionally, though, the same name is used.

The unit of currency in Russia is the rouble.

The dollar – which takes its name from a sixteenth-century Austrian coin called a thaler – has become a widely used name for many coins. The USA, Canada, Australia, Fiji, Hong Kong and others all have dollars as their currency.

BITS AND QUARTERS

A thaler coin.

European settlers in America had very little money. They were not allowed to mint their own coins, so foreign coins were used instead. The most common were the large silver Spanish dollars called 'pieces of eight'. To make them into small change, they were chopped into quarters, or into eight wedge-shaped pieces called bits. The names 'bits' and 'quarters' are still used in the USA.

This colourful banknote is from Argentina.

Today making coins is a high-tech business. The Royal Mint in Britain produces 2,000 million coins a year, over half of them for 60 other countries around the world. The USA has four mints in Denver, Philadelphia, San Francisco and West Point, New York.

US currency being printed.

People who wish to pay for goods from another country must pay in a different currency. In France, the currency is the franc, in Germany, the deutschmark. In Mexico, the peso is used, and in Japan, the yen. Currencies of other countries can be purchased at a foreign exchange.

Travellers abroad often need to carry large amounts of money. They might need to pay for hotels, or car hire, or a sightseeing trip. Before they leave home, they can visit their bank or foreign exchange and buy special travellers' cheques, which can be exchanged, when they arrive, into the currency of the country they are visiting. This is a much safer way to carry money because travellers' cheques can only be signed by the person who bought them.

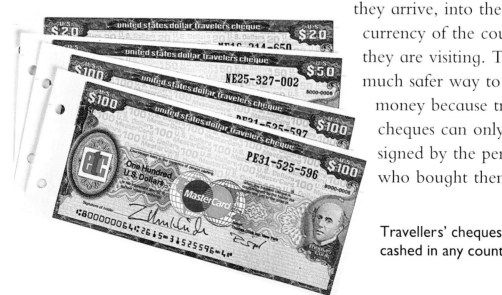

Travellers' cheques can be cashed in any country.

Right: This foreign exchange chart shows the value of currencies in £ sterling.

FOREIGN EXCHANGE CAMBIO WECHSELSTUBE DEVISES ETRANGERES		
Currency	We Sell	We Buy
AUSTRIA	2.00	2.14
CANADA	2.00	2.14
FRANCE	8.36	9.06
GERMANY	2.50	2.67
GREECE	300.00	310.00
ICELAND	98.00	116.00
KENYA	102.00	131.00
MEXICO	4.37	5.63
NEW ZEALAND	2.50	2.70
USA	1.50	1.54

Different currencies all have different values. If you are travelling in Greece, where the currency is the drachma, you might decide you want to buy, say, a T-shirt which costs 3000 drachmas. But first of all you need to know how much 3000 drachmas is worth in your own money; the T-shirt might be cheaper to buy at home.

The exchange rate compares currencies of different countries against each other.

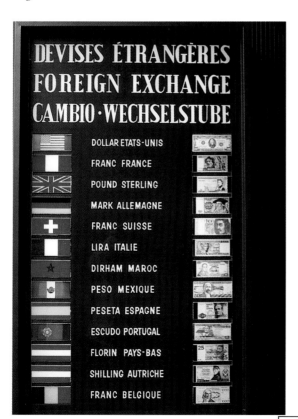

Discover from the chart (above) how much 3,000 drachmas is worth, and decide whether the T-shirt is a good buy (because currency values change all the time, the chart shows exchange rates from 1994, and will now be out of date).

Banks and travel agents usually display up-to-date exchange rates. Have a look at one of their charts to find out what changes have been made since this chart was made.

You can see that there are as many different types of money in the world as there are nations, regions and peoples. This will continue to be the case as long as people trade with each other. How do you think money will change in the future?

TIMELINE

3500 BC In Britain flint is used in exchange for goods.	**2500 BC** Copper rings used in Egypt as money.	**2000 BC** Trade routes being set up around the world.	**1850 BC** Mesopotamians use metal weights as money.	**1800 BC** Bronze rings used as money in northern Europe.
1400 BC Cowrie shells used as money in China.	**750 BC** Tiny pieces of electrum used as money in Lydia, Turkey.	**690 BC** First coins made in Lydia.	**500 BC** In China coins are made in the shape of tools.	**400 BC** Cast copper weights are used as money in Olbia, Russia.
336 BC First coin bearing a ruler's head is struck in Thrace, Turkey, honouring Alexander the Great.	**44 BC** Julius Caesar is stabbed to death; a coin is later issued.	**AD 650** Issue of earliest paper note, T'ang Dynasty, China.	**1066** In Britain the value of 'sterling silver' is set (sterling means something that can be relied on).	**1368** During the Ming Dynasty in China, paper money is widely used.
1400 Copper rings, known as manillas, used as money in Nigeria.	**1500** Handwritten paper banknotes first used in Europe.	**1609** Bank of Amsterdam founded.	**1661** The Swedish Stockholm Bank issues the first printed bank note in Europe.	**1694** The Bank of England is established.
1848 Gold discovered in California and three years later in Australia.	**1923** Runaway inflation in Germany makes money almost worthless.	**1946** The World Bank and International Monetary Fund set up to support world banking.	**1961** First computerized banking introduced at Chase Manhattan Bank, New York.	**1973** The USA abandon the gold standard as the main way of valuing the dollar.

GLOSSARY

Alabaster Soft, white, almost see-through stone, often made into jars, vases and ornaments.

Bank account Money held in a person's name at a bank.

Cast Metal heated and left to cool in a certain shape.

Chieftain A leader.

Circulation The amount of money going round.

Flint Very hard stone that can be sharpened to have a cutting edge.

Goldsmith A person who made gold articles and also worked as a banker.

Guarantee An assurance that an object is what it claims to be.

Hides Animal skins.

Intricate Complicated and difficult.

Mint The making of coins, or the place where coins are made.

Oasis Fertile area in a desert.

Ornate Highly decorated.

Panning The washing of gold dust from crushed rock - a process used by gold miner.

Symbol Something used to mean something else.

Supply The amount being used.

Tarnish Lose its shininess.

Trade To buy, sell or exchange goods.

FURTHER READING

'The World of Work – Bank' by Jenny Vaughan (Macmillan, 1989)

'Money – Eye Witness Guides' by Joe Cribb (Dorling and Kindersley, 1990)

'Money through the Ages' by Catherine de Sairigne (Moonlight Publishing, 1991)

'World Coin Encyclopedia' by Ewald Junge (Hutchinson, 1984)

'Gold and Gold Hunters' by Lance Salway (Kestrel Books, 1978)

PLACES TO VISIT

Bank of England Museum
Threadneedle Street
London EC2R 8AH
England

Museum of Victoria
328 Swanston Walk
Melbourne VIC 3000, Australia

The Currency Museum
245 Spark Street
Ottawa ON K1A OG9
Canada

INDEX

Numbers in **bold** indicate subjects shown in pictures as well as in the text.